THE SIXTH

Garfield

TREASURY

THE SIXTH

Garfield

TREASURY

BY: JIM DAVIS

BALLANTINE BOOKS • NEW YORK

Copyright © 1991 United Feature Syndicate, Inc.

The Sunday strips appearing here in color were previously included in black and white in *GARFIELD Goes to Waist, GARFIELD Hangs Out, GARFIELD Takes Up Space*, and *GARFIELD Says a Mouthful*.

All rights reserved under International and Pan-American Copyright Conventions. Published in the United States by Ballantine Books, a division of Random House, Inc., New York, and simultaneously in Canada by Random House of Canada Limited, Toronto, Canada

Library of Congress Catalog Card Number: 91-91884

ISBN: 0-345-37367-6

First Edition: November 1991

10 9 8 7 6 5 4 3

OH, VERY WELL, GARFIELD, YOU MAY HAVE MY STEAK

I KNOW. I'M A SUCKER FOR THE LOVING ADORATION OF A PET

© 1989 United Feature Syndicate, Inc.

1-29

JIM DAVIS

© 1989 United Feature Syndicate, Inc.

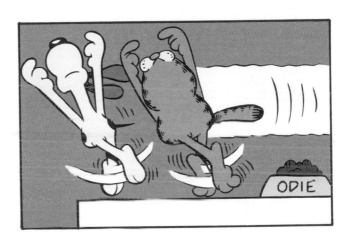

3-19

JIM DAVIS

© 1989 United Feature Syndicate, Inc.

4-2 JIM DAVIS

I DON'T KNOW WHAT GOT INTO MY CAT! I'M REALLY SORRY!

NONSENSE! THAT'S THE MOST EXERCISE REBA'S HAD IN YEARS!

© 1989 United Feature Syndicate, Inc.

MUNCH
MUNCH
MUNCH

MUNCH
MUNCH
MUNCH

JIM DAVIS 4-30

WOOSH WOOSH WOOSH
WOOSH WOOSH
WOOSH

WHY CATS ARE LAZY...

CAT'S POINT OF VIEW

© 1989 United Feature Syndicate, Inc.

WHY CATS NEED HELP..

CAT'S POINT OF VIEW

WHY CATS HATE DOGS...

CAT'S POINT OF VIEW

JIM DAVIS   5-14

AND WHY CATS ARE VAIN...

A CAT'S FAVORITE VIEW

JIM DAVIS

7-2

WHAP!

JIM DAVIS 8-13

JIM DAVIS

9-3

10-1 JIM DAVIS

ZWIP!

IT'S ALL IN THE WRIST

JIM DAVIS

10-15

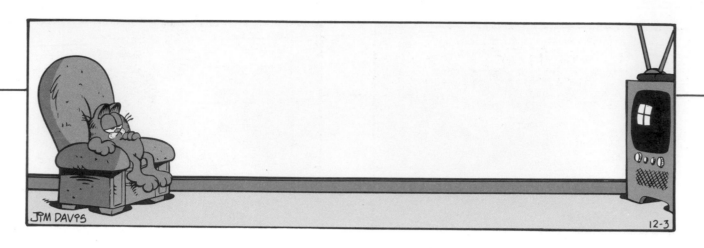

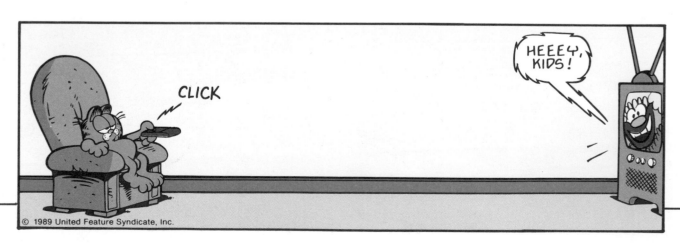

NOW WHILE I'M BUSY BEING THE LIFE OF THE PARTY, YOU SIT IN THE CORNER AND DO WHATEVER IT IS CATS DO

YES, SIR

JIM DAVIS 12-31

HEY, HEY! HERE COMES "MR. PARTY ANIMAL"!

HEY, EVERYBODY!

DID ANYBODY HERE ORDER 2000 PEPPERONI PIZZAS?!

WHO AM I? AND WHERE DID I GET THIS RUBBER CHICKEN?

WATER BALLOONS AT FOUR O'CLOCK

I LOVE THE WAY THIS CHIP DIP SQUISHES BETWEEN MY TOES! HEY! TURN DOWN THOSE CHAIN SAWS!

ARE YOU HERE FOR THE HUMAN SACRIFICE?

WE LOVE YOUR CAT!

WANT HIM?

© 1990 United Feature Syndicate, Inc.

JIM DAVIS

1-7

JIM DAVIS

SHOOF

SHOOF

SHOOF

ALL RIGHT! ALL RIGHT!! I'LL FIX YOUR BREAKFAST!!!

1-14

© 1990 United Feature Syndicate, Inc.

THE MIGHTY LION LIES IN WAIT...

HE SPIES A HERD OF EGGS OVER EASY!

THEY BECOME SKITTISH, SENSING DANGER...

HE STRIKES!

THE VILLAGE DAM BURSTS, SENDING ORANGE JUICE GUSHING THROUGH THE MELEE!

© 1990 United Feature Syndicate, Inc.

JIM DAVIS 2-11

CAN'T I HAVE A NORMAL BREAKFAST?

SUDDENLY HE HEARS THE RUSTLING OF TOAST IN THE BUSH!

JiM DAViS

2-25

© 1990 United Feature Syndicate, Inc.

JIM DAVIS

3-25

GARFIELD, I'M HOME!

JON'S NOT GOING TO LIKE THIS

JIM DAVIS 6-17

© 1990 United Feature Syndicate, Inc.

JIM DAVIS 7-1

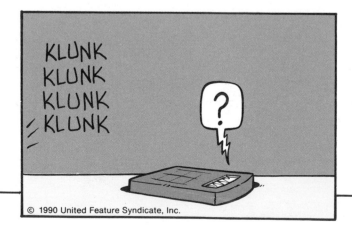

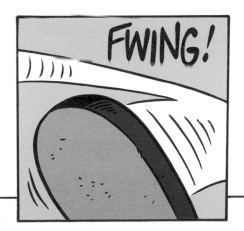

JiM DAViS 10-14

10-21   JIM DAVIS

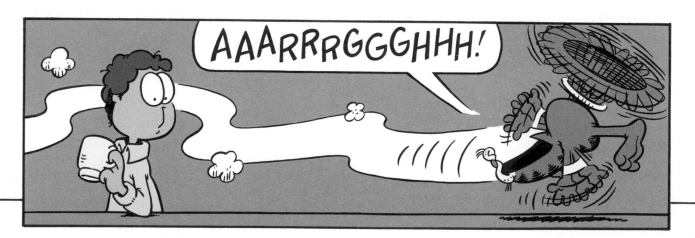

THAT'S IT! I'M TIRED OF US NEVER AGREEING ON WHICH TV SHOW TO WATCH

YOU CAN WATCH THE BEDROOM TV AND I'LL WATCH THE LIVING ROOM TV

© 1990 United Feature Syndicate, Inc.

JiM DAViS 11-25

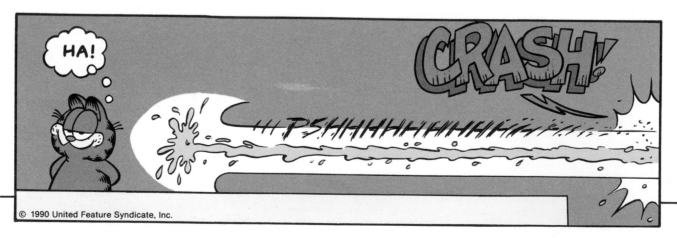

© 1991 United Feature Syndicate, Inc.

JIM DAVIS 1-13

STRIPS, SPECIALS OR BESTSELLING BOOKS...
GARFIELD'S ON EVERYONE'S MENU

Don't miss even one episode in the Tubby Tabby's hilarious series!

BIRTHDAYS, HOLIDAYS, OR ANY DAY…

Keep GARFIELD on your calendar all year 'round!

GARFIELD TV SPECIALS
__BABES & BULLETS   36339/$6.95
__A GARFIELD CHRISTMAS   34368/$6.95
__GARFIELD GOES HOLLYWOOD   34580/$6.95
__GARFIELD'S HALLOWEEN ADVENTURE   33045/$6.95
  (formerly GARFIELD in Disguise)
__GARFIELD'S FELINE FANTASIES   36903/$6.95
__GARFIELD IN PARADISE   33796/$6.95
__GARFIELD IN THE ROUGH   32242/$6.95
__GARFIELD ON THE TOWN   31542/$6.95
__A GARFIELD THANKSGIVING   35650/$6.95
__HERE COMES GARFIELD   32012/$6.95
__GARFIELD GETS A LIFE   37375/$6.95

BALLANTINE SALES
Dept. TA, 201 E. 50th St., New York, N.Y. 10022

Please send me the BALLANTINE BOOKS I have checked above. I am enclosing $ .... (add $2.00 for the first book and 50¢ for each additional book to cover postage and handling). Send check or money order—no cash or C.O.D.'s please. Prices are subject to change without notice.

GREETINGS FROM GARFIELD!
GARFIELD POSTCARD BOOKS FOR ALL OCCASIONS.
__#1 THINKING OF YOU   36516/$6.95
__#2 WORDS TO LIVE BY   36679/$6.95
__#3 GARFIELD BIRTHDAY GREETINGS   36770/$7.95
__#4 BE MY VALENTINE   37121/$7.95
__#5 SEASON'S GREETINGS   37435/$8.95

Also from GARFIELD:
__GARFIELD: HIS NINE LIVES   32061/$9.95
__THE GARFIELD BOOK OF CAT NAMES   35082/$5.95
__THE GARFIELD TRIVIA BOOK   33771/$5.95
__THE UNABRIDGED UNCENSORED
  UNBELIEVABLE GARFIELD   33772/$5.95
__GARFIELD: THE ME BOOK   36545/$7.95
__GARFIELD'S JUDGEMENT DAY   36755/$6.95
__THE TRUTH ABOUT CATS   37226/$6.95

Name _____

Address _____

City _____ State _____ Zip Code _____

Allow at least 4 weeks for delivery   3/90 TA-267